The Pursuit of Excellence

Your Call To Operate In Greatness!
~In Business & Ministry~

Jamal D. Moore

(The Pursuit of Excellence)

Copyright © 2015 by (Jamal D. Moore)

ISBN (978-0692606315) **JD Moore Enterprises LLC**

Printed in USA
Book Cover designed & Photo Edits by: Bobby Barnhill
Photo credit: Teresa Wall Photography
Editing by: Lita P. Ward, LPW Editing Services

Dedication

I want to dedicate this book to my beloved mother Josephine Moore (deceased) who instilled in me at a young age to pursue my dreams, and to always do my best on any task. To my father Randolph Moore who pushes me to achieve greatness, and to always remain humble. And to so many who have inspired me and provoked me to fulfill my God-given purpose.

~ JD Moore

Table of Contents

Preface

"Don't blink you'll be finished reading this book before you have dinner. Everyone who knows me understands and appreciate that I' m not a "long winded speaker". Well same thing goes in writing. (Laugh out loud). I mean I understand that the human mind only can adsorb so much information, and our attention span can go so fast no matter how intrigued we are there is a line to draw for a stopping point. So you all enjoy the book.

About The Author

Jamal Donnell Moore is the CEO of JD Moore Enterprises LLC. A motivational speaker, servant of God, an author, and future business mogul, Moore's passion is fueled by God. Owning several businesses Jamal's entrepreneurship is demonstrated extensively through his passion and ambition in life. Jamal is an assistant minister of music at his church Harvest Time Evangelistic Outreach, and serves faithfully under the Leadership of Pastors Charles & JoAnn McCullough.

JD Moore is the youngest of his seven siblings and feels bless to be a part of such a loving close-knit family. Moore graduated from high school with honors received various awards and was inducted into the National Honor Society. Jamal also served as the Vice President of the Christians United Fellowship of Students. Moore is a *member of the Washington's Young Professionals where he actively serves in any area needed. He is currently in college studying business administration. Moore has had the pleasure and privilege of managing two major retail stores at an early age.*

JD Moore lost his mom at age 16 and he is very passionate about young children who lose their family members. Moore is known for his approach of short and sweet, his "don't blink" approach is hilarious and unique. A man with true humility and one who knows what it's like to struggle, and knows that without God he would be nothing. JD Moore has used his platform to glorify God and has set him up to reach many people nationally and internationally via social media and abroad. Moore plans to travel the world see all of God's beautiful creations and touch as many lives for the kingdom as possible.

JD Moore wishes to inspire uplift and encourage as many people as possible.

Jamal is excited about his future and looking forward to finding his wife, so he can enjoy life, be fruitful and multiply. His favorite quote is" your destiny is not tomorrow; your destiny is today"!

Introduction

I am writing this book because I am passionate about seeing God's people excel in life. I want to share some practical principles to maximizing your best life now by pursuing excellence; choosing to go above and beyond what is asked of you. It's more than just about seeing people do well, but also helping others realize what we have been called to. We live in a world where so many try to fit in but God created us to stand out and be an example to the world. When we operate in greatness and pursue excellence then we are giving glory to God our Father.

Too often we count ourselves out of God's best for our lives. We allow doubts, fears, and discouragement to bind us, limits us and convince us to settle where we are. Well, not anymore! I hope this book inspires you to be great in all your endeavors and provokes you to rise above the mediocre lifestyle. I pray that the nuggets found in here by many great people in the world who have gone before us to make the crooked path straight will bless you. And to realize that we don't have to reinvent the wheel, we just need to get in God's will and plan for our lives. Success leaves clues and I intend on finding them in the pursuit of excellence.

Chapter One

Exceed Expectations

Hey you! When was the last time you visited a business or church and after your dealings and experience with them you thought, "WOW?" Exactly! It's that feeling you get when you thought you were going to experience or see less, but instead they went above or beyond what you expected.

Here are two things that come to mind. Once you have been exposed to a new level of excellence, you can't keep it to yourself. You are eager to share your personal experience with others. Yes it was that darn good and who knew that they did that there. Another is you think when is the next time I can come back again.

Maybe you were surprised by the way the waitress handled your order. Or the way the ushers and greeters welcomed you and walked you to your seat to make you feel special. Now naturally everyone expects you to be nice but it's the things they didn't expect that had their minds like, "Wow this is how it should be."

Now I'm writing to share with you how this journey can put us right in the place where we need to be. Everyone likes to experience the "wow factor" every now and then. But as a business, ministry or individual, operating in excellence can bless you tremendously. In anything that you do, you must use Godly wisdom, and seek Him in all things. We don't pursue excellence to bring glory to ourselves but rather that God may be glorified in everything we say and do.

Jesus told them to do more than what's expected, carry it two miles"; that's the attitude we need to have. I'm not just going to serve in my church, but I' m going to put my heart into it for the work of the ministry. I'm a person of excellence; I go above and beyond what's asked of me.

Joyce Meyer once said, "Excellent people exceed expectations." In other words, they go the extra mile, they do more than is asked, and they take extra steps to ensure the highest quality. If people were to describe your work, would excellence come to mind or simply mediocrity? Meyer declared, "You can run into mediocrity accidentally but you have to purpose to be excellent." Thus, exercising minimal effort will lead to a mediocre performance at best, but really going above and beyond the call of duty takes a conscious effort.

I'd like to think that God loves to exceed our expectations even far beyond what we can fathom. The Bible tells us in the book of Ephesians 3:20 KJV, "Now unto him that is able to do exceeding abundantly above all that we could ask for or think, according to the power that worketh in us." So according to our faith we can expect God to exceed our expectations, go above and beyond what our little minds can even ask for or think. No we are not God nor will we ever be Him. But we should expect him to move miraculously in our businesses, ministries, and lives. Why not believe God for it to work in us and through us? Thus the pursuit of excellence begins.

I believe that in our pursuing of excellence, it will bless us real good; however in using it, you must start out like you can hold out. And no matter what level we are on, we must operate in doing business well. The Bible tells us in Romans 12:11 that we are not to be slothful in business; fervent in spirit; serving the Lord. So everything that we have and do, God's expectations are that we do it very well. Notice He didn't ask us to be perfect, because He knows we are imperfect people serving Him. But He does ask us to do our best with what we have been given. In every task assignment we are to handle it in such a way that it pleases God. We must see the importance of being a good steward over everything that He has entrusted us with.

We are already God-minded people so we've already been anointed to walk in excellence. As the famous quote goes "the blessing is sure." I dare you to take one moment to declare out loud now "The Blessing Is Sure!"

If you have ever operated in any level of excellence you know and understand that it may not have been easy to always do but it is certainly necessary. When people come in contact with you they look for your level of expertise to kick in. That's why they visit your church, and when they come, do they experience all that was marketed to them? Or do they leave with the feeling of, "Well the flier was nice, but it just wasn't what I expected or the level of service was just

sloppy and unorganized." We don't want to
be responsible for a bad taste in someone's
mouth but rather the sweet flavor that keeps
them hooked and coming back.

You Can Do It

Excellence is not a hard task to
achieve, but like anything else it requires
effort and putting your all in it. I don't care
who told you that you would be nothing or
you would not amount to anything. Truth be
told, these same people are telling you this
in hopes that you will agree with their
statement and settle for mediocrity. They
want you to live like this so they can feel

secure in themselves because they know and see your potential.

But I come to tell you that you can rise above it all and choose to live a life of excellence. You can start your own business, you can write that book, and be a bestselling author. You can start and grow your ministry. You can serve others with excellence; you can give your all to a job or career. You can climb the corporate ladder and become the CEO of a Fortune 500 company. You can do it all because with Christ in your life you have the ability and resources needed to be great in any endeavors you choose.

Your hater's and enemies are never far, which is a good thing because they have to be close if they're going to become your footstool. You'll catch that last statement at lunchtime. Whether you're doing good or bad things, you are going to be talked about and criticized. So why not choose to be great at what you do. It doesn't matter if you are cleaning restrooms or if you're teaching in the pulpit, do it as unto the Lord and execute it with excellence.

Growing up in a family of four siblings and not having the best living conditions, our parents always instilled in us to do our best to whatever we put our hands to do and watch God bless it. Even though I was the baby of the family, as I got older, I began getting all the workload on me. Jamal do this and Jamal do that. Being humbly submitted to my parents, I always did as I was told. Not because I was trying to be the best, but because I was submissive to them because they had authority over me. My parents knew if they ask me to do a job, I wouldn't be sluggish about doing it. Whether I had to wash dishes or take out trash, I always put forth my best effort on any task. Then finally I discovered that the reason why they kept asking me to do something is because I wouldn't just do what was asked of me, but I went above and beyond what was expected of me.

For example, if my mom told me to take the trash out of her room, I would empty her trash, wipe the can down and put a new bag in it for them. I even went as far as to check every other room in the house to see if trash needed to be emptied and would do the same for those. These same traits grew up in me and stayed with me and for every task that I did, I put forth my best effort.

Like many people, my family was always looked down upon because of what we didn't have. We didn't fit their criteria to be accepted. So we were told you'd never be anything, have anything or amount to anything. But God gets the glory and the devil has been proven a liar again. In 2013, I started a freelance business creating marketing products and services for churches and businesses. In 2014, I launched it as a sole proprietor business, and 25,000 copies were printed on the front page of Washington Daily News. The business grew to an office, which I currently work from now. I am a home CEO having no overhead cost. My customer retention is great because God is faithful and continues to bless the work of my hands. Great is His faithfulness towards us! You can do it too. Greatness lies in you, so let's get started on our road to destiny.

Chapter Two

Be Consistent

"This Book of the Law shall not depart from your mouth, but you shall meditate on it day and night, so that you may be careful to do according to all that is written in it. For then you will make your way prosperous, and then you will have good success" (Joshua 1:8).

My pastor, Charles McCullough preached a message entitled "Stick with it." Now this message stood out to me because in everything that we do we must be willing to stick with it. I told you earlier that you must start off like you can hold off. What people experience in your ministry or business they will continue to expect it. So on this journey to excellence, we must commit to doing well and growing in what we do. We go from faith to faith and glory to glory, so from here we got to go higher!

I want to point out some things in this scripture above. It says that this Book of law shall not depart out of your mouth. So ultimately what you put in you will stick with you, but watch the clause, "but you shall meditate on it day and night." We must want it so bad that we meditate on it; we're constantly thinking on it. "Finally, brothers, whatever is true, whatever is honorable, whatever is just, whatever is pure, whatever is lovely, whatever is commendable, if there is any 'excellence,' if there is anything worthy of praise, think about these things" (Philippians 4:8 ESV).

My colleague in the gospel Niko Peele once wrote, "Favor opens doors but excellence keeps you in." Think about that for a minute. One, two, three, fifty-nine! Okay, catch up already! (laugh out loud)

I mean really the favor of God will open up many doors for you, but it's your consistency that keeps you in them. But we have to be committed to all that is written in it, and stick with it. "For then will you make your way prosperous and have good success" is what the Scripture says. Now I don't know about you but I think we all would like to experience more success.

In our journey to being consistent, please note that one of the simplest things that come to our mind is what is most important to others. Here are a few examples; keeping the same telephone number for the duration of your existence. I can't stress enough how something so simple can hurt your image's brand and name. Another issue is keeping your website up-to-date. You want to always have a reason for people to constantly want to visit your site, and if you're not going to keep it up-to-date, it is probably better that you not have one. Let me pause right there for a moment.

With my first business, I created a website and was all excited about it. But as time went on, I didn't update it with my latest sales and pertinent information. So after a couple of bad incidents with a few respected clients, I realized that if I weren't willing to stick with it, then I would need to take it down. Sometimes what you aren't willing to tend to will hurt you. So this second time around in my pursuit to excellence, I will not be defeated. So challenge yourself to commit and change for the better. After all, we have different destinations but we must commit to our efforts in excellence if we want to be a winner.

You're Going to Win

By no means do I despise small beginnings because you have to start from somewhere, and no matter where you start, if you will commit to excellence, whatever it is that you're doing you will win. You can start small and still have big dreams and visions. If you keep your vision in front of you and stick with it, put your dreams into actions, then you will see your vision fall into place. Jim Carey the famous actor kept a check in his pocket for 10 million dollars, even though he didn't have a dime to his name and was living in a car. But he stayed committed to his plan of action and today he is one of the wealthiest actors. God will super-size your vision if you dare to believe Him.

So many people get frustrated and get lost along the way because they have what we call fabricated success, the appearance of looking successful but are messed up. We have to be okay with where we are now and how we start out; not comfortable but content. Look you're already a winner because you took the step to commit to something and doing it well. I hear it said all the time, "If it was easy then everyone would do it," and that's true. But the simple fact that you have set out to become better in whatever it is that you do is an indication that you're on the winning side.

You and I are winners; we were designed to be the head and not the tail, above and not beneath, the lender and not the borrowers. When you see yourself winning, you will act like a winner and everyone around you that's not winning will be influenced to come up with you, if they decide to commit to excellence. But if not, I advise you to leave them alone. We can't allow anyone to sabotage our winning streak.

I see you winning in your home, in your businesses and at your ministry. Everyone around you is being provoked to do well. We can't go under for going over. We are victorious on every side and we have what it takes to make a mark on this generation!

Chapter Three

Distinguished
Flaws and All

"Then this Daniel became distinguished above all the other presidents and satraps, because an excellent spirit was in him. And the king planned to set him over the whole kingdom" (Daniel 6:3).

Pastor Joel Osteen made a great point with this passage of Scripture. He said, "Notice it didn't say God distinguished him and he got promoted. It says Daniel distinguished himself." That's a good reason to strive for excellence because it will set you apart from everyone else.

No, you and I aren't perfect but operating in a spirit of excellence will set you apart from the rest. The Bible said that Daniel had an excellent spirit in him. Most of us already have a spirit of excellence in us, but we must look past all our hang-ups and hiccups to operate and flow in them. This spirit does not care if you are tall, short, fat, skinny, ugly and busted or disgusted. However, it requires us to put our trust in God and that we totally rely upon Him to get the job done. In Him we live move and have our being. It is the undisputed grace of God that allows us to operate so gracefully.

Daniel didn't operate in excellence because he wanted people to notice him, but he did it because he looked to the God that was on him. He couldn't help but carry things out a certain way. It might not have been popular but it was with purpose to bring glory to God! "Whatever you do, work heartily, as for the Lord and not for men" (Colossians 3:23). "Show yourself in all respects to be a model of good works, and in your teaching show integrity, dignity" (Titus 2:7).

Also, we want the reward that God has for us and not man, because God gives us His best. "Rendering service with a good will as to the Lord and not to man, knowing that whatever good anyone does, this he will receive back from the Lord, whether he is a slave or free" (Ephesians 6:7-8). Matthew 6 says, "Take heed that you do not your alms before men to be seen of them: otherwise ye have no reward of your father which is in heaven."

"Do you see a man skillful in his work? He will stand before kings; he will not stand before obscure men" (Proverbs 22:29). Your gift will make room for you and bring you before great men (Proverbs 18:16). His gifted spirit distinguished Daniel, and so will ours! So get ready for doors to open up and for blessings to come down.

Everyone has a gift that God has placed in him or her, and whatever that gift might be, it is imperative that we work to perfect our gift. The time will come when your gift will be used, and you want to make sure that you're ready to flow in it. Preparation time is never wasted; we need this time to work on us so when the opportunity presents itself, we will have no problem walking in it with confidence.

Excellence does not necessarily mean the absence of mistakes, but it does mean the presence of faith and determination. To be excellent at whatever God has called you to do, you must first ask for His strength to accomplish the task and then, secondly, His endurance to complete it. Daniel was met with obstacles in his endeavor to serve the Lord wholeheartedly, but he remained steadfast to the course of action he believed the Lord set for him to take.

Don't get caught up trying to be a perfectionist when pursing excellence for you will set yourself up for failure. There is a huge difference between trying to be perfect and endeavoring to be excellent. Trying to be perfect is an impossible task, and one I wouldn't suggest you do.

Remember we're on the road to pursuing excellence.

There are many people in life and in the bible who we can refer to who didn't have the best situation but embraced their gifts and used them for the glory of God. For example, check out Albert Einstein. He was four years old before he could read but that didn't stop him from becoming a theoretical physicist. Einstein even had speech challenges, but he was able to tap into his gifts regardless of his impairments. Moses the chosen one was sent by God to deliver the Hebrews out of bondage. God set him in a place where he learned excellence, even though he didn't speak well, but that didn't stop God from using him to deliver the people out of Egypt.

When we decide to carry a spirit of excellence with us wherever we go, it will be distinguished and will stand out from the crowds in any environment, or any place we have the opportunity to influence others for good. Anita Brooks says, "In order to become irreplaceable a difference must be evident." Darren Dake adds, "Work from your passion. Giving all your energy is different than giving all your potential." We're not trying to become irreplaceable, but rather have the perspective that how we operate and run things causes our efforts to stand out, by maximizing all of our potentials.

I know we all have challenges in life but we must not let our flaws dictate our destiny, but embrace the path that is laid before us. It is then that we find a way to take a bad situation and make the best out of it. If you're an entrepreneur you know that when life throws you lemons, you make lemonade. We must understand that we are uniquely designed and put together. There is no one like you and no one can beat you at being you. My pastor said one time he asked the Lord why you want me to start a ministry when there are already a lot of churches already. God told him that he wasn't there. You see you would be amazed at what your own style and personality can bring to a place. But you won't know if you don't go. You'll never find out if you don't apply for that manager position, or to serve on the greeter's team or to serve in children's church. The job doesn't make the difference; we make the difference!

Now I'll be honest, but I'm only sharing it with you. Can you keep a secret? Well, I started a business that required having typography and proof reading skills. Guess what? I'm not good at typing or proof reading, but it didn't stop me from launching my first business, Moore's Office Solutions. I wouldn't let that defeat me, so where I lacked in an area, I outsourced jobs or just simply asked for help. As you grow, you can hire people to do things that you're not good at to be a blessing to your company. Don't allow your flaws to stop you! One significant aspect of our flaws is that they have a way of keeping us humble. But that's another story for another time. Keep calm and carry on in your pursuit of excellence.

Chapter Four

Create a Standard

Excellence is a standard worth committing to. People will do business with you just because they like you. You may not be the best or offer the cheapest price, but because you're likeable you are able to sell yourself. Your uniqueness will set you apart from the rest in a saturated market. But don't settle for being just likeable; pursue excellence, and ask God to bless the works of your hands.

How can they follow unless there are leaders? In business and ministry, we must create content and properly execute it well through our staff and team members and or individuals. We've got to show up and deliver; this is exactly what our staff expects from us. If we have no vision, the people perish. If we don't know where we are going, how can we expect someone to follow us?

On day one, we must make it clear on what we want to do when we want to do it and how we are going to accomplish it. Faith without works is dead and it's hopeless for us to talk about something and don't put any action behind it. First and foremost, we must assemble our team. "Every good organization has a team because nothing really great can be accomplished alone," states Bishop T.D. Jakes. We must delegate and give proper and clear instructions. A person's job can be a lot easier when they know what is expected of them. In our pursuit here are some things that we can work on:

- Job descriptions; they not only tell us what is expected but it also lays out details of regular duties, working relationships as to who they are accountable to and job qualifications.

- And last but not least, which I think is mostly important, training and development.

Excellence requires that we stay relevant and live in our now. If we want to get where greatness lies, then we must do what is required of us to stay in the game. You can easily be out of the game and not know it. One thing I learned in business school is though you don't put your focus on your competition and surroundings, you should always know what they are up to and doing. This is not to say you're going to do everything they do because excellence is not being a copycat, but it's staying creative and ahead of the game.

Joel Osteen said, "If you're not growing, improving, and learning new skills, then you are falling behind." This year I attended a marketing seminar conducted by Pastor Aaron McNair Jr. and he said something that stood out to me and I quote, "You must always stay creative, because once you stop, someone is catching up with you." I thought that to be the most profound statement because we are in a society where nothing stops for two seconds anymore. I mean every six months to a year, the latest phones, technology and social media platforms are coming out. And if you're not careful to stay informed, then you will find yourself stagnant, unfruitful and left in the dark ages. That's one of the pluses with having youth around; you can always count on them to know the latest trend. Now I' am not suggesting that you have to follow everything, but you should know of it and how it could help or bless your organization.

On day two, not only should we be investing in ourselves but in the people who invest in us. There are many ways to do this. Increase their level of exposure in business, from expos, to seminars and classes. Also you can send them to keynote conferences that will not only challenge their intellect, but ignite the spark that will cause a blazing fire. Get everyone excited and involved.

My pastor tells us all the time if you don't stand for something you will fall for anything. That's why they have instilled in us the importance of being on time, which for us is before time. If you are thirty minutes early, you're on time, and if you're on time then you're late. We must teach ourselves the importance of showing up before time, and holding that standard. For example, what would happen if service starts at 7:00pm sharp and you show up at 7:00pm sharp. Yet your job is to play the keyboard and the keyboard isn't working properly. Well you have a problem because now you're fumbling in front of everybody trying to handle a situation that could have been avoided had you shown up thirty minutes prior to service. Or let's say you're the greeter, but you show up at 6:55pm, and service starts at 7:00pm. Not only do you look unprofessional, but half of your guests are already in and seated. So, who are you greeting? I'm just giving practical examples that could hinder us on our journey to achieving excellence. Mediocre and nonchalant attitudes must be set aside; it is imperative that we operate at our best.

Let me hit the businesses. If our company hours state 9:00a.m. – 5:00p.m. Monday through Friday, then everyday there should be someone their prepping to open up on time. The last impression you want to give any customer is that you are sloppy by being late and unorganized. I remember when I was employed at Food Lion as a cashier. The store would open up at 7:00a.m. and we would already have a customer in line waiting to check out, but the office manager didn't have the tills in the drawer ready to go. This really got on my nerves, but humbly I stood there and talked with the customer until around 7:05a.m. until the manager came out. Not only did she have to put the till in the drawer, but had to enter in manager's code to loan the money to the register. I want you to understand that I wasn't mad with anyone, but it really bothered me to see this happen in a retail chain store on such a large scale. Little did I know that because of the spirit of excellence inside of me which said, "When I become an office manager, I'm going to make sure all registers are filled with tills, so even at 7:00a.m., we would be able to service our customers promptly and efficiently," that's exactly what happened once promoted, with the help of God. No, I wasn't perfect, but through that it provoked every other office manager to do the same when opening the store. Not only that, but people took a great notice of how one little simple thing made everything run so much smoother. Once you create a standard, you are bound to flow with greatness in other areas of your life. Our proclivities toward creating a standard must be kept in order to take us to that next level. Don't let anything stand in the way of you giving your best towards everything.

Chapter Five

The Bar

"Without pursuing excellence, life will remain bland, very vanilla, and lukewarm at best. The quest for excellence fuels our fire and keeps us from just drifting downstream gathering debris..." excerpt from the author J. Hampton Keathley, III. Well said sir!

The pursuit of excellence comes from doing our best with what we have to the glory of God. Biblically speaking, our pursuit is doing the best with the gifts and abilities God gives us. For every good and perfect thing comes from above. God doesn't want us to have excellence so we can be arrogant and draw attention to ourselves. But He wants us to operate in it so He can say, "Look at my sons and daughters doing what they were created to do through excellence."

A while ago my church was going through some changes with our media and sound department. So we had someone come in and train the sound technicians on how to properly work the sound booth and flow with the service. For years we had done things the same in the mindset of "if it's not broken don't fix it." Well the particular example I want to point out is the booth is located in a dark corner that has light because of the room's illumination. So during the training, the trainer suggested that they put a light over the soundboard so they could see every knob. Now keep in mind for years we had never had this, but this trainer had to come along and challenge us or set the bar higher to add a light over the board.

To make a long story short, once one of the brothers installed the light over the board it brought much more light that we never knew we needed. I'll even go as far to say that we didn't know we were in the dark until we added the light. We literally saw a huge difference on the board that has helped us go to another level in ministry just because a bar was set and we met up to it. A great commodity that came out of this training, but had our sound technicians not been teachable then we would have incurred problems. When you operate in excellence you are always able to learn something that can be beneficial to you and your organization.

Excellence might not be popular but it's certainly needed in everyday life to bring balance and some stability to our public structures and organization. You can't pick and choose where excellence should be used. For example, you expect for the president to wear proper attire to meet with other world leaders, but in your business you meet with new customers in jogging pants. Yes, setting the bar is what is necessary to reach our invisible goal. The bar isn't a stopping point for us but it's an indication that we are making progressive strides to attainable goals. Let's say you give your staff a bar and tell them that this month we want everyone to show up 45 minutes before each service. Well you put it out there and those who strive to follow the ministry's expectations will follow suit.

When creating the bar we should create a reality bar where everyone can reach it in efforts to do well. We should want to see everyone and everything excel around us and do well. When one goes up, we all go up. However everyone won't see a need to but that shouldn't stop us from dreaming. Joseph set the bar high as he began to share his dreams to his family. One fact we know to be true, everyone won't support you in your efforts to be great.

Excellence Costs

1 Corinthians 15:58 says, "So then dear brothers and sisters, be firm. Do not be moved! Always be outstanding (doing over, above and excelling) in the work of the Lord. Knowing that you labor is not in vain in the Lord!"

The pursuit of excellence sometimes will mean hard work and diligence, which may take on various forms—research, study, time, sweat, planning, brainstorming for ideas, etc. It may well mean going against something bigger than you, and sometimes navigating through tough situations in life. Thus, in keeping with our own shortcomings and weaknesses, the pursuit of excellence in the execution of our daily routine or special projects is something that must be pursued by God's strength. Such a mentality can be seen in the attitude and actions of the Apostle Paul. As one totally committed to God's purpose for his life, Paul gave his all to be all God wanted him to be in seeking to bring men to maturity in Christ, but he did so by God's enablement rather than by his own strength.

Paying the price may very well mean showing up early and leaving late. You have to be willing to pay the price if you're going to be a cut above the rest. There are different levels of excellence and the higher you go, the more you grow. Don't get caught up in trying to be great overnight; God Himself didn't even try to finish the earth in one day. He took six days to complete his masterpiece, and on the seventh day He rested. Your labor is not in vain. You can't expect to have more and keep doing less; you won't receive better results doing the minimum trying to just get by.   The famous quote goes, "If you always do what you've always done, you'll always get what you have always gotten." Let no man fool you; you have exactly what it takes and it is only through God that we are able to do so!

Because we know that with God all things are possible to them that believe!

Chapter Six

You are Extraordinary

It's no secret that from our mother's womb we were born with purpose, not to be ordinary but extraordinary. Only time and working of our gifts will cause us to tap into our extraordinary potentials.

Our call to excellence:

- 1 Corinthians 12:31 – "But covet earnestly the best gifts: and yet shew I unto you a more excellent way."

- Proverbs 12:26 - "The righteous is more excellent than his neighbor: but the way of the wicked seduceth them."

- Proverbs 17:27 – "A man of understanding is of an excellent spirit."
- Philippians 1:10 – "That ye may approve things that are excellent; that ye may be sincere and without offense till the day of Christ."

People don't follow ordinary; they follow extraordinary. It's simple. What can you or what are you adding to society? Are you here just to breathe the air in for your oxygen? If your business or ministry were to close today, what would people think?

Would you be missed from the community or would you just be a thought in the moment and people never remember your presence or existence. Take a few moments and think about that.

Extraordinary people add something; they're the solution to a problem. Pastor Aaron McNair Jr. said, "If you don't add anything, then you are considered a zero." We all know no matter what you add to a zero, you're going to always get what you add to it and nothing more. So basically extraordinary has value; it's able to add something to the equation.

Our church once set up an after school program and our tag line was "Making a mark that can't be erased." That's exactly what excellence does; it causes a mark to be made in businesses, ministries and communities that will always be remembered. One thing I can say about our church is that wherever we go to visit, we stand out. It's not that we're better, but we're not ordinary; a spirit of excellence has been

instilled in us. We're always there thirty
minutes before the services start, and
sometimes we beat the home church to their
ministry. Not to be seen, but our church has
established a standard that we not only use
when were home but when we go off to
visit. What you learn home should follow
you elsewhere. Our commitment to this has
provoked others to do well.

A Choice to Pursue Excellence and Integrity

For many individuals, mediocrity is a
normal lifestyle they chose to do as little as
possible just to get by. In actuality, it was
never God's plan for us to be mediocre or
average. He doesn't just want His children
to get by or do what everyone else does.

God has called us to be a cut above to bring glory to Him in every aspect of our lives.

When we chose to be a person of excellence and integrity, it changed our scope. Everything we do is intentional and with purpose. That may mean we will have to keep our word even when it's difficult or not in our favor; arriving to our destinations on or before time, and sometimes staying late. An excellent spirit will show up in the quality of your work and the tone in which you do it.

If we want to live at our best now, we must start aiming for excellence and integrity; choosing to work honestly and efficiently and doing a little bit more than we are required to. We can't get caught up in "well, everybody's doing it" kind of attitude. Yes, our colleagues might be late; yes they might play around when the boss is not looking. But we are not like them; we are ambassadors and representatives of God and anything we do bears a reflection on Him.

Even down to what we drive and I'm certainly guilty of this. Sometimes our cars may be dirty on the outside as well as the inside. You know from the front to the back the car is filled with office clutter, junk food and etc. But when we take the time to clean it before we go out, not only does it makes us feel better, but we actually look better. Our image is important not because of what we have or want to please man, but it pleases God. Extraordinary people will be a good steward of what they drive even if you think it's a clunker.

Even your appearance and dress attire are all packages that pursue excellence. See ordinary people don't see a need to clean up the old car, and you and I both know that's why God won't bless them with a new one. For the bible declares that if we are found faithful over a few things then He will make us rulers over many.

Are you willing to pay the price to do the right thing? Like paying those bills on time, making the best business decisions and being truthful when negotiating deals? How can God trust us with millions if He can't trust us to do right with the hundred? Yet too many of us will let these little things keep us from going up higher.

One of my pet peeves in business is to conduct business with a ministry and they not honor their words, or expect that they can pay you any time as long as you get it. And for some, you may never get it if you don't have a contract with them or collect it upfront. I had a customer one time ask me to make a flyer for their church project. So in good faith I did it and over delivered on my end. I kid you not; the people who I made this transaction with decided that it was okay to pay me an entire month later. And the sad thing is that the invoice was less than $25.00. So being young and fairly new to the business, this taught me to establish some guidelines upfront as to how I would be paid. On bigger transactions, I even required a deposit on the order because people won't see importance on something unless it requires an investment from them first. Just like when you go to the bank and apply for a loan, the bank wants to know how much of your own money or assets you are willing to put into the deal.

In business and ministry, there is no room for cutting corners. Our integrity is on the line, not just with man but ultimately God. For God knows even the intent of the heart. So before you think about cutting corners to make a little extra money, you should realize that God is always watching. Remember everyone and everything belongs to God, whether they confess it or not so we must be careful in our actions and follow through with all truth.

Chapter Seven

Don't be Excellent

By Yourself

Sometimes it feels good to know that you're the only one doing something well or better. But don't you think it's selfish to keep all of what you know to yourself? When God blesses us with knowledge and wisdom, we are obligated to share it. For it's not about us, but it's about advancing the kingdom and His business. No matter how you acquired the information you obtained; you should always be open to impart your learning. Now I' am not suggesting that you have to share it for free, because there are many people who make a living by hosting seminars, conferences and even consulting sessions. However, the main point is that you should be willing to help others when you can. After all, we are our brother's keeper and when we see something that could be done better and we have the know-how and the time to share, by all means do it.

On this quest the more you learn and grow, the more the people around you should learn and grow. It has been said before that a leader should duplicate their selves to be successful. What's on our leaders should come on us involuntarily.

Bishop T.D. Jakes said it like this, "Don't be great by yourself, because you diminish your impact. Great people can accommodate the greatness of others without being intimidated by their greatness." Think about how many businesses and or ministries you have in your network. Now think about how many of them operate in excellence and how many of them which do not, but you can offer a helping hand to. One truth is that no one person knows everything about any topic, but when we share our thoughts with others, we can feed off what each of us as individuals can offer. The Bible says iron sharpens iron.

Expose yourself to new levels of excellence, because you can't evolve to what you're not exposed to. Imagine as a young child growing up, you are exposed to many careers. You're not really sure what's all involved in each job but you have an idea of what you think it is that a certain profession does. You then begin to make a decision as to whether you would gravitate to it or not. But had you not been exposed to it you would have never known about it. You can't become what you didn't know existed.

I remember in third grade they had the fire department to come visit our school. My friends and I were so excited and anxious to see them. On that day, they brought all of their equipment with them, even a training trailer. The men and women were so informative and shared with us with enthusiasm. After training was over, some of my classmates were going back to the class saying, "I'm going to be a fireman when I grow up." Now whether or not they went into that profession, they had a better understanding when they left. Some of us simply don't do better because we aren't exposed to a better way of doing things.

In closing, follow your instinct for excellence; be known for doing things well.

On this journey to achieving excellence, don't allow anyone to tell you that you don't have to do all of that. Surround yourself with people who challenge and provoke you to do better, have better and know better. In doing so, you will be respected and admired.

We don't have time to waste. Excellence is calling and asking if you are willing to take this journey and answer the call in business and ministry. Laid-back lifestyles are over; no longer is mediocrity accepted, but from here everything must go to a higher level and be done in decency and in order.

Finally, I want to encourage you and tell you that you have what it takes to achieve excellence! You and I were not created to be average. Whether you are a servant in ministry or the leaders, the employees on the job or the CEO of the company, you and I were called to excellence and the gracious hand of God will gracefully execute our pursuit.

Hello Friends! Did you enjoy the book?

I would love to hear from you!

Jamalmoore300@gmail.com

Or visit WWW.JAMALDMOORE.COM

Let's stay connected follow me on social media!

@JDmoore and Jamal D. Moore.

Be blessed, and pursue excellence!

J. D. Moore ENTERPRISES LLC.

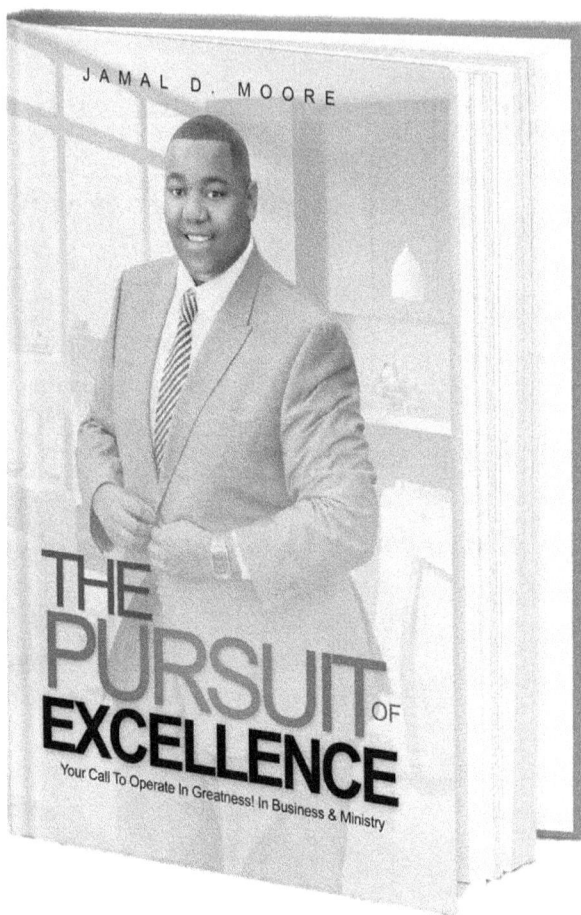

Tell someone about the book!

Write your review online at www.amazon.com

Twenty-One Affirmations

I hope you have enjoyed this book, but I want to do something that Jesus did! Now you might ask, "Jamal what did Jesus do that you're going to do?" Well, if you give me a second I will tell you.

Jesus said I'm not going to leave you comfortless, and neither am I! So in the spirit of excellence, I've included twenty-one affirmations that you can declare over your life for the next 21 days!

I promise you it's going to bless your life; short, sweet and to the point. Let's get started speaking the blessing over your life!

Are you ready? Let's Go!!!!!

Day 1

Lord, I thank you for the gifts that you have

entrusted with me. I am intentional about using

everything that you invested in me for Your glory!

Day 2

I am great because I know that You live on the inside of me. I choose to shine my light in every aspect of my life.

I win!

Day 3

I am not who they say I am. I choose to believe

what Your word says about me!

I am victorious!

Day 4

Today I choose to live better.

Today I choose to serve better.

Today I choose to give better.

Today I become a better me.

Day 5

Thank you God for blessing the

works of my hands.

All my endeavors are blessed.

My future is bigger, brighter, and better!

I am intentional!

Day 6

My life is a reflection of Jesus!

People don't see me, but the God in me!

My life will inspire others!

Day 7

I am anointed.

I am gifted.

I am humble.

I operate in excellence!

Day 8

I am committed to excellence.

I understand that I have been called to operate in

greatness!

Day 9

I inspire others to be great.

I choose to help everyone see the importance of

excellence in life.

Day 10

I will push pass the fear of failure.

I will succeed.

I am distinguished.

There is something in me that the

world needs.

Day 11

I am consistent.

I am productive.

I am fruitful.

Day 12

The blessings of God are sure!

Day 13

I will overcome any and every obstacle that I

will have to face, because God already wrote

victory in my life!

Day 14

God's plans for me are that I prosper

and be in good health!

Day 15

I am the head because God says I am.

The favor of God is on my life!

Day 16

Where there is vision,

God will make provisions!

No more room for excuses; just results!

Day 17

I am too productive to worry about what

negative people have to say.

Day 18

I am significant and relevant!

I lead people into a place of power!

Day 19

I choose to maximize my potential.

I go above and beyond what is

asked of me.

Day 20

I am not average.

I am a cut above the rest.

I am blessed!

Day 21

I am receiving the best out of life now.

I am excited about the person that

I'm becoming!